Symphony No. 94
in G Major
"Surprise"

Joseph Haydn

DOVER PUBLICATIONS, INC.
Mineola, New York

CONTENTS

Symphony No. 94
in G Major
"Surprise" (1791)

One of the composer's last twelve symphonies (nos. 93–104)
—known collectively as the London Symphonies—
written for the Salomon Concerts in London (1791–95).

INSTRUMENTATION

2 Flutes [Flauti, Fl.]
2 Oboes [Oboi, Ob.]
2 Bassoons [Fagotti, Fag.]

2 Horns in C, G [Corni, Cor.]
2 Trumpets in C [Trombe, Tr-be]

Timpani [Timpani, Timp.]

Strings [Archi]:

Violins I, II [Violini]
Violas [Viole]
Cellos & Basses
[Violoncelli e Contrabassi, Vc. e Cb.]

Symphony No. 94

in G Major

"Surprise"

I

II

22 (II)

III
Menuetto

Menuetto da capo

IV
Finale

34

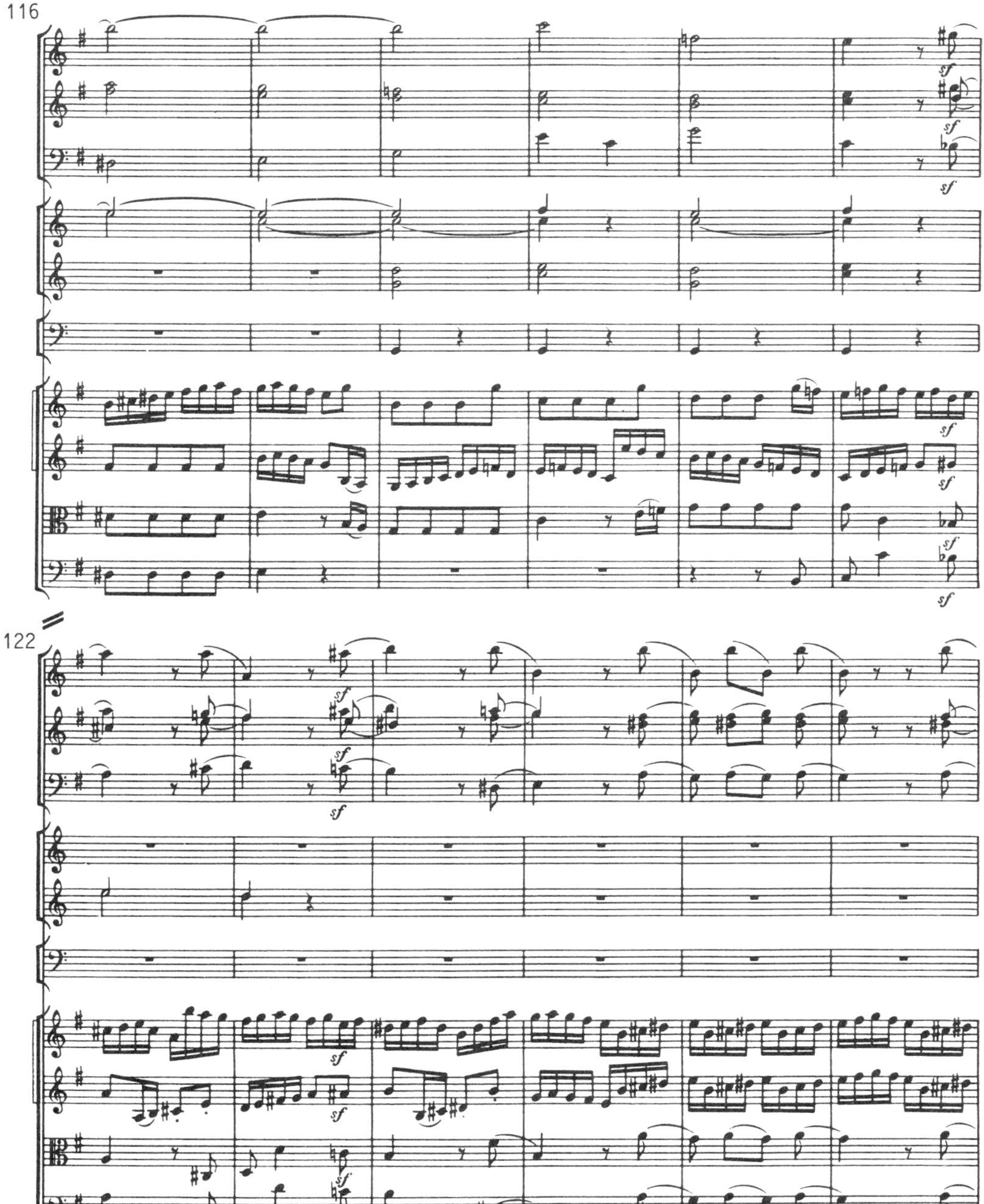
116
122
sf

128

134

160

166

DOVER FULL-SIZE ORCHESTRAL SCORES

THE SIX BRANDENBURG CONCERTOS AND THE FOUR ORCHESTRAL SUITES IN FULL SCORE, Johann Sebastian Bach. Complete standard Bach-Gesellschaft editions in large, clear format. Study score. 273pp. 9 x 12. 23376-6 Pa. **$12.95**

COMPLETE CONCERTI FOR SOLO KEYBOARD AND ORCHESTRA IN FULL SCORE, Johann Sebastian Bach. Bach's seven complete concerti for solo keyboard and orchestra in full score from the authoritative Bach-Gesellschaft edition. 206pp. 9 x 12. 24929-8 Pa. **$11.95**

THE THREE VIOLIN CONCERTI IN FULL SCORE, Johann Sebastian Bach. concerto in A Minor, BWV 1041; Concerto in E Major, BWV 1042; and Concerto for Two Violins in D Minor, BWV 1043. Bach-Gesellschaft edition. 64pp. 9⅜ x 12¼. 25124-1 Pa. **$6.95**

GREAT ORGAN CONCERTI, OPP. 4 & 7, IN FULL SCORE, George Frideric Handel. 12 organ concerti composed by great Baroque master are reproduced in full score from the *Deutsche Handelgesellschaft* edition. 138pp. 9⅜ x 12¼. 24462-8 Pa. **$12.95**

COMPLETE CONCERTI GROSSI IN FULL SCORE, George Frideric Handel. Monumental Opus 6 Concerti Grossi, Opus 3 and "Alexander's Feast" Concerti Grossi—19 in all—reproduced from most authoritative edition. 258pp. 9⅜ x 12¼. 24187-4 Pa. **$13.95**

LATER SYMPHONIES, Wolfgang A. Mozart. Full orchestral scores to last symphonies (Nos. 35–41) reproduced from definitive Breitkopf & Härtel Complete Works edition. Study score. 285pp. 9 x 12. 23052-X Pa. **$14.95**

PIANO CONCERTOS NOS. 17–22, Wolfgang Amadeus Mozart. Six complete piano concertos in full score, with Mozart's own cadenzas for Nos. 17–19. Breitkopf & Härtel edition. Study score. 370pp. 9⅜ x 12¼. 23599-8 Pa. **$16.95**

PIANO CONCERTOS NOS. 23–27, Wolfgang Amadeus Mozart. Mozart's last five piano concertos in full score, plus cadenzas for Nos. 23 and 27, and the Concert Rondo in D Major, K.382. Breitkopf & Härtel edition. Study score. 310pp. 9⅜ x 12¼. 23600-5 Pa. **$16.95**